Asthma

Dr. Alvin Silverstein,

Virginia Silverstein, and

Laura Silverstein Nunn

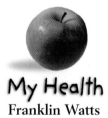

My Health
Franklin Watts

A Division of Scholastic Inc.

New York • Toronto • London • Auckland • Sydney

Mexico City • New Delhi • Hong Kong

Photographs © 2002: Peter Arnold Inc.: 38 (Martha Cooper), 23 top, 24 (David Scharf), 31 (SIU), 19 (Volker Steger), 15 (Erika Stone); Photo Researchers, NY: 9, 35 (John Bavosi/SPL), 21 (Charron/Jerrican), 4, 28 (Mark Clarke/SPL), 13 (Brian Evans), 40 (Guy Gillette), 11, 33 (Damien Lovegrove/SPL), 23 bottom (Oliver Meckes), 25 (Kent Wood); Stock Boston/Margaret Ross: 34; Superstock, Inc.: 17; The Image Works: 22 (Spencer Ainsley), 39 (Dick Blume/Syracuse Newspapers), 26 (Bob Daemmrich); Visuals Unlimited: 8 (John D. Cunningham), 10 (Michael Gabridge), 32 (SIU), 6 (Inga Spence).

Cartoons by Rick Stromoski

Library of Congress Cataloging-in-Publication Data

Silverstein, Alvin.
    Asthma / by Dr. Alvin Silverstein, Virginia Silverstein, and Laura Silverstein Nunn.
        p. (cm).—(My Health)
    Includes bibliographical references and index.
    Summary: Discusses asthma, its causes and treatments, and emphasizes what can be done to maintain personal health and prevent asthma attacks.
    ISBN 0-531-12048-1 (lib. bdg.)   0-531-16637-6 (pbk.)
    1. Asthma—Juvenile literature. [1. Asthma. 2. Diseases.] I. Silverstein, Virginia B. II. Nunn, Laura Silverstein. III. Title. IV. Series.
RC591.S55 2002-02-19
616.2'38—dc21   2001004966

Contents

Out of Breath

Take a deep breath and let it out. Usually you don't have to think about taking a breath. In fact, you may not even realize you are doing it. Breathing becomes noticeable when you are running to catch a bus or sick with a cold.

Some people, however, have to think about breathing every single day. Sometimes they have to struggle just to take a breath. These people may have **asthma**.

Asthma is a condition that causes part of a person's airways (breathing passages) to become narrow, making it hard for air to get through. As a result, the person may have trouble breathing and may cough or wheeze. Tiny bits of dust, mold, or pollen in the air may

Did You Know…

Asthma is a common condition and affects 12 to 15 million Americans. About 5 million of those affected are children.

◀ **Sometimes it can be difficult to catch your breath.**

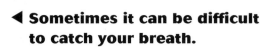

5

bring on breathing problems. Air pollution, very cold weather, exercise, or even a bad cold can also make it hard to breathe.

Asthma attacks can be very dangerous—even deadly. There is no cure, but there are ways to keep asthma under control. Symptoms can be treated with fast-acting medications. There are even some things that you can do that may prevent asthma attacks from occurring.

Sometimes people with asthma have trouble breathing when they exercise.

How Breathing Works

Before you can understand what happens during an asthma attack, first you need to know how normal breathing works.

When you breathe in, or inhale, air comes in through your nose and mouth. The air then passes down into two spongy organs in your chest called **lungs**, which fill up with air, like balloons. Inside the lungs, oxygen—an invisible gas that is part of the air—passes into your blood, which carries it to the many cells of the body. Your body needs oxygen to produce the energy you need to run, play, eat, think, and even sleep. When the cells use oxygen to produce energy, they also make a gas called carbon

Did You Know...

You breathe as many as 20,000 times each day.

Breath 'O' Meter

20,000.00

7

dioxide. The blood carries carbon dioxide to the lungs, and it is pushed out when you breathe out, or exhale. When you breathe in again, the process is repeated and it brings fresh air into the lungs.

The parts of the body involved in breathing make up the **respiratory system**. The respiratory system looks a lot like an upside-down tree. The air you breathe goes down your throat (the **pharynx**) and through your voice box (the **larynx**) and continues down the main breathing tube, or **trachea**. You can feel the trachea at the front of your throat. Then the

Many different body parts work together to help your respiratory system function properly.

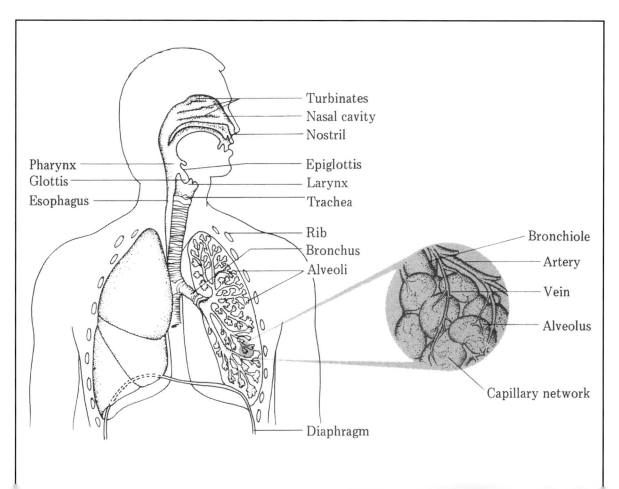

Turbinates
Nasal cavity
Nostril
Pharynx
Glottis
Esophagus
Epiglottis
Larynx
Trachea
Rib
Bronchus
Alveoli
Bronchiole
Artery
Vein
Alveolus
Capillary network
Diaphragm

air goes through two large tubes (**bronchi**), which lead into the lungs. The bronchi branch into smaller, almost threadlike tubes, called **bronchioles**, which look like the branches of a tree.

The bronchi and bronchioles are wrapped in bands of muscle. When these muscles relax, the airways widen. When they contract, or tighten, the airways narrow and less air can flow through. Normally when you breathe, these muscles are loose and relaxed.

The bronchioles lead into millions of tiny balloon-like air sacs in the lungs called **alveoli**. They look

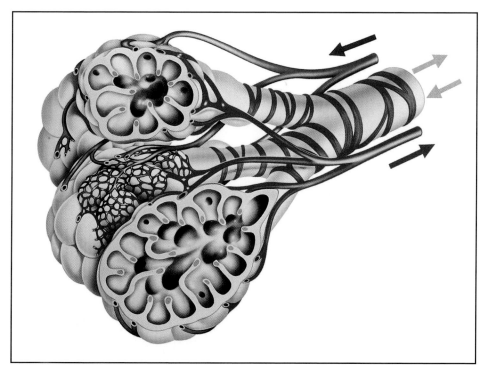

Alveoli look very much like a bunch of grapes.

like tiny bunches of grapes, but they are too small to see without a microscope. This is where the exchange of oxygen and carbon dioxide takes place.

The airways have built-in defenses to protect the lungs from foreign particles that may be breathed in from the air. Some particles that enter your nose get trapped in bristly hairs inside your nostrils. Anything that gets past this first line of defense falls into a gooey fluid called **mucus** that covers the lining of your nose. Mucus is also produced in the airways, and it picks up pollen grains or tiny bits of dust that might have gotten through. Some of the cells lining the airways have tiny hairlike structures called **cilia**

Hairlike cilia line your airways and move particles away from your lungs.

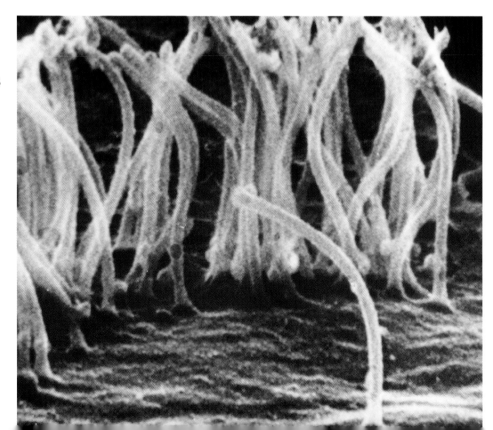

that move back and forth, creating waves in the mucus coating. Like a conveyor belt, the moving mucus sweeps trapped particles up and away from your lungs. The particles leave your body when you blow your nose, sneeze, or cough.

Wind Power

When your lungs are working properly, you can blow air out of them with as much force as the winds in a hurricane. You may think you're blowing hard when you're blowing out the candles on a birthday cake, but the gust of air from a cough or sneeze is even harder. When you sneeze, air explodes out of your airways at a speed of 100 miles (160 kilometers) per hour. The air from a cough travels at 500 miles (805 km) per hour!

Air quickly shoots out of your airways when you sneeze.

What Is Asthma?

The term *asthma* is a Greek word meaning "panting." It was first used thousands of years ago to describe the wheezing sound that people make when they are having trouble breathing.

People with asthma have very sensitive airways that tend to overreact when foreign substances are breathed in. Doctors sometimes refer to these airways as "twitchy."

Who Gets Asthma?

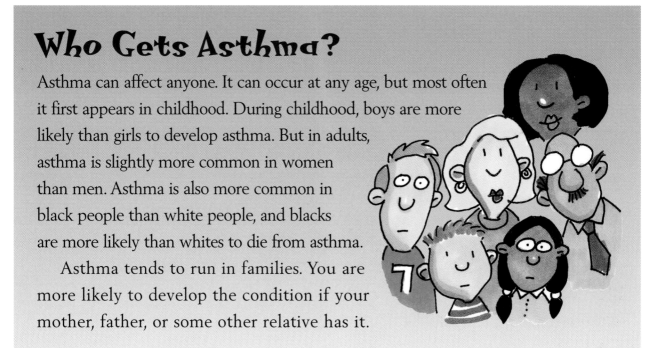

Asthma can affect anyone. It can occur at any age, but most often it first appears in childhood. During childhood, boys are more likely than girls to develop asthma. But in adults, asthma is slightly more common in women than men. Asthma is also more common in black people than white people, and blacks are more likely than whites to die from asthma.

Asthma tends to run in families. You are more likely to develop the condition if your mother, father, or some other relative has it.

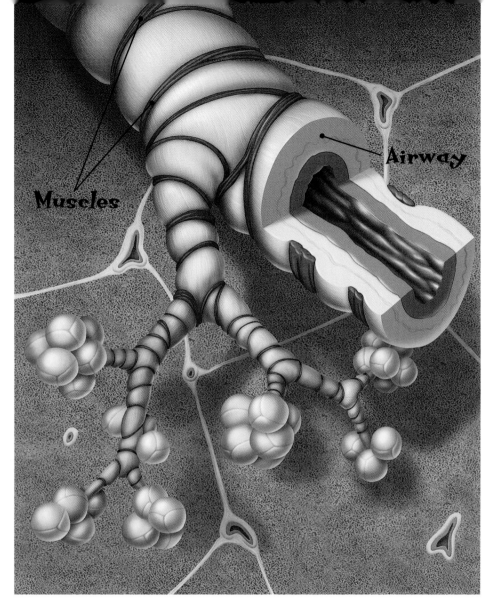

Muscles

Airway

Muscles wrap around the respiratory airways and cause them to constrict during an asthma attack.

What happens during an asthma attack? When the bronchial tubes are exposed to things like smoke or dust, they become irritated. This causes the muscles that wrap around the airways to tighten and prevent the particles from getting farther into the lungs. The contracting muscles make the airways narrower, leaving less room for air to get through. This effect is called a **bronchospasm**.

At the same time, the walls of the bronchial tubes become **inflamed** and swollen, making it even harder for air to flow through them. The inflammation also causes the airways to produce a lot of extra mucus. Sometimes the mucus forms plugs in the airways, which blocks them even more.

When the airways are constricted, breathing becomes difficult, and a person may become short of breath. **Wheezing** is the most obvious symptom of asthma. When air tries to squeeze through the narrow passageway, it makes a whistling sound. But not all people with asthma wheeze, which may make it hard to identify the condition. Some people feel their chests getting tight because their lungs have to work harder than usual to push air through the narrow airways.

Did You Know...

People with asthma do not have a problem with breathing in, but rather breathing out. When the air comes in, it gets trapped, and a person with asthma has to struggle to push the air back out of the narrow airways.

OUT

Coughing is very common in people with asthma.

Coughing is the most common symptom of asthma. It may be caused by the extra mucus produced in the airways. Bronchospasm alone can also cause coughing. Unfortunately, people usually don't see coughing as a sign of something serious such as asthma. They may think it is caused by a cold or that something is in their throats.

Asthma symptoms vary greatly from person to person. Whether the symptoms are mild or severe depends on how seriously the airways are inflamed.

It is important to treat asthma attacks early. This helps to prevent further inflammation that can make the symptoms worse. If asthma is not treated right away, the attacks may destroy some of the cilia that sweep particles away from the lungs. Then, with fewer cilia, the airway lining cannot clear out the particles as effectively.

Activity 1: Asthma *Is* Like Breathing Through a Straw

Did you ever try breathing through a straw? Many asthma patients say that is what it feels like when they are having an asthma attack. You can do a little experiment to get an idea of what it's like to have asthma. All you need is a straw and a watch or clock with a second hand.

Run in place for 2 minutes, timing yourself with a watch or clock. When the time is up, pinch your nose and put a straw into your mouth. Then try to breathe in and out **only through the straw.** Now, narrow the straw by pinching it in the middle. *Is* it even more difficult to breathe? This is what it feels like when a person with asthma tries to breathe during an asthma attack.

What Causes Asthma?

No one is sure exactly what causes asthma. Scientists do know that there are certain things in the environment that can bring on the symptoms of an asthma attack. These things are called **triggers**. An asthma attack usually occurs in a person either right away or within about 15 to 30 minutes after that person is exposed to a trigger.

Asthma is very often linked with allergies. An **allergy** is an unusual reaction to a substance that is normally harmless. Most people can breathe in

Most people can play with animals because they are not allergic to them.

the summer air or play with a puppy without sneezing. But for people with allergies, these kinds of things may trigger an asthma attack.

Usually you get sick when germs get into your body. Your body has many defenses against germs. The body's defenders, the **white blood cells**, are called in to fight these foreign invaders and protect you from further harm. The white blood cells are jelly-like blobs that can swim easily through blood and squeeze between body cells. They are part of your **immune system**.

Did You Know

Allergies are involved in about 90% of children with asthma. But people with allergies do not necessarily develop asthma.

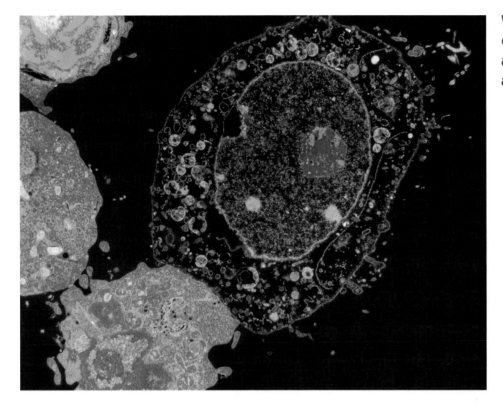

White blood cells are attacking a germ.

Some white blood cells go after germs and attack them. Others make special proteins called **anti-bodies**, which may damage the germs or make them easier to kill.

After the battle is over, some of the antibodies stay in the body. If the same kind of germs invade again, the cells that make antibodies will quickly make a whole new supply so they can fight the germs. As a result, the person will not get sick from the same kind of germs again. The person is now immune to that illness.

Are You Too Clean?

Some health experts say that one reason why more and more people are developing allergies and asthma may be that the environment is much cleaner today than it was years ago. House dust contains germs. Exposure to germs helps children to build up immunity to diseases. When children are exposed to a lot of germs early in life, their body defenses get stronger. Their immune systems also learn to react less to harmless things. But children may not be able to develop an effective immune system in an environment that is too clean.

People with allergies have an immune system that is a little too active. It makes antibodies against chemicals that would not have caused any harm. These may be chemicals on the surface of dust or pollen grains (tiny powdery particles that flowers use to make seeds), or chemicals in foods. A substance that causes an allergic reaction is called an **allergen**.

You may not get a reaction the first time you are exposed to an allergen. If you eat a strawberry, for instance, your body may mistake it for an invader and produce antibodies, but there won't be enough of them to bother you. The next time you eat strawberries, your body produces more antibodies. The more strawberries you eat, the worse your allergy symptoms will become. This kind of exposure build-up is called **sensitization**. Your body has now become sensitive to strawberries, and you will have an allergic reaction, such as an itchy rash or a stomachache, every time you eat them.

Pollen grains from flowers can cause an allergic reaction.

In an allergic reaction, histamine may make the eyes itchy and watery.

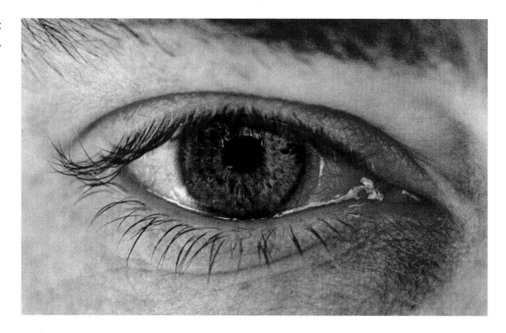

During an allergic reaction, sensitive cells in various parts of the body (such as the skin or the breathing passages) react to the presence of allergens and allergy antibodies. These body cells send out a chemical called **histamine**. Histamine's job is to fight invaders, but it can also cause annoying symptoms, such as a runny nose, watery eyes, itching, and sneezing. Pollen is a very common trigger for people with asthma. Many people have seasonal asthma and have attacks during the "hay fever season."

Other allergens include house dust and molds, which can be found all over your house. They can be under mattresses, in closets, in carpets, or in stuffed animals.

What's in House Dust?

If you put a tiny bit of dust under a microscope, you might be surprised at what you see. House dust may include a variety of things: fibers from bed sheets, flakes of dead skin, pollen grains, pet hair, mold spores, and little bits of insects. These kinds of things could be enough to make you sneeze, but an allergy to dust may actually be caused by **dust mites**. These are tiny bugs that feed on dead skin flakes and other things in dust. It's usually the dust mites' droppings that cause allergy problems. They are so tiny and light that they can easily float through the air, enter your nose, and cause symptoms.

Some places in the world are asthma-free. For instance, asthma is very rare among the Eskimos in North America. That might be because the climate is too cold for dust mites to live.

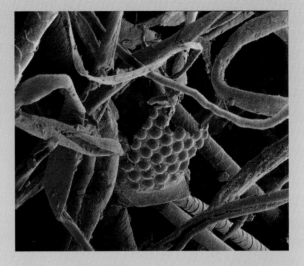

This dust ball contains an insect eye, cat and human hair, and cotton fibers.

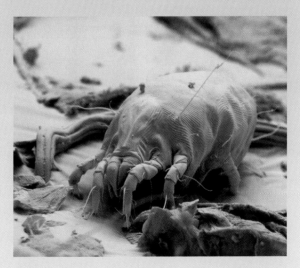

Dust mites cannot be seen without a microscope.

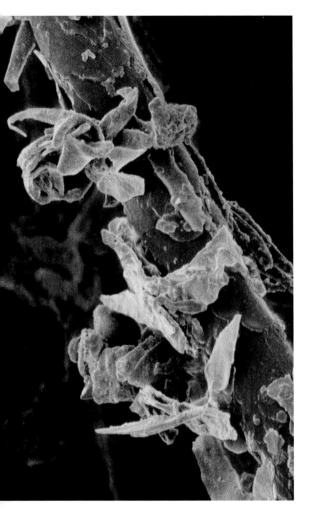

Dog hair and dander can collect on furniture and carpets.

A person who develops asthma symptoms after petting a cat or dog may be allergic to animal **dander**, tiny flakes of skin. Animals shed dander on carpets and furniture. Different animals have different dander, so you may be allergic to dogs but not to cats. The feathers of birds also contain allergens. Mice, hamsters, and guinea pigs can be a problem as well, but the allergen from these animals is mainly in their urine. Many people are allergic to the chemicals in cockroach droppings. In cities, wild mice, rats, and cockroaches are a big cause of asthma.

Foods can bring on an asthma attack. Common food allergens include milk products, fish, peanuts and other nuts, wheat, and eggs.

Other asthma triggers may not be related to an allergy. For instance, a person with asthma may be sensitive to irritating substances—things that can bother anybody, not just someone with allergies. These include air pollution, cigarette smoke, and certain chemicals in products.

The Dangers of Smoking

Everyone knows that smoking cigarettes is bad for you. When you breathe in cigarette smoke, the harmful chemicals in it—such as carbon monoxide—go right into your lungs. Carbon monoxide is very dangerous because it keeps the blood from bringing oxygen to the brain, heart, lungs, and other important organs in the body. Cigarette smoke also damages the cilia in the lining of the airways. Eventually, they are unable to sweep mucus and foreign particles out of the lungs and up toward the throat. Some chemicals in cigarette smoke stay in the lungs. They can cause some serious illnesses, such as bronchitis, emphysema, or lung cancer. If these things can happen to a person with healthy lungs, can you imagine what smoking can do to someone with asthma?

Studies have shown that smoking is not only bad for the smoker. It is also harmful to anybody who is around that person. Secondhand smoke—the smoke that people around a smoker breathe—can be very dangerous for someone with asthma. Smokers who have children with asthma should never smoke around their children. Even smoking in the same house can leave harmful chemicals that can linger for hours.

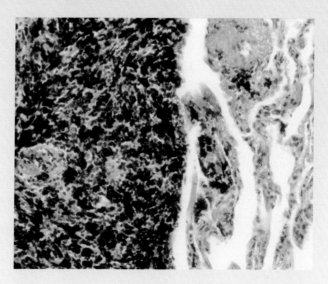

This smoker's lung is covered with black tar on the left side of the photograph.

A respiratory illness, such as a cold or flu, can also trigger an asthma attack. Cold weather, stress, and even crying or laughing can set off an attack.

Exercise is a common trigger for people with asthma. When people exercise, their muscles use up extra oxygen. So, their lungs work harder, breathing faster and taking in more air. During exercise, the nose does not have enough time to warm up the air before it goes to the lungs. The air may be cold and dry when it gets to the lungs. The cold air entering the airways may make them suddenly get narrow. As dry air passes through them, the airways lose the moist mucus that normally protects them. Since people with asthma have very sensitive airways, cold, dry air is more likely to bring on an attack.

Exercise is a common asthma trigger.

Activity 2: How Do the Airways Dry Out?

Run the tip of your tongue over the roof of your mouth and note how moist and slippery it feels. Then breathe in and out through your open mouth (holding your nose closed) for 30 seconds. What does the inside of your mouth feel like now?

When you exercise, a lot of air flows in and out through the airways. So, their moist lining dries out quickly. Here's an experiment to show you how this happens.

Wet two sponges and squeeze them out just enough so that they are not dripping. Place one wet sponge in front of a blowing fan but keep the other one away from the flow of air. Observe each sponge every 5 minutes. (Look at them, feel them, and press a piece of paper towel gently against the surface of each one to see if it picks up a spot of moisture.) Note how long it takes for the surface of each sponge to get dry. You will find that the one you placed in front of the fan will dry out more quickly than the one outside the air current.

How Do You Know It's Asthma?

Asthma can be pretty tricky to detect. Many of its symptoms—coughing, wheezing, shortness of breath, chest tightness, and breathing problems—may be confused with signs of other respiratory conditions.

Symptoms of asthma, such as coughing and wheezing, can often be confused with other illnesses.

Asthma symptoms are also different in different people, and they may be mild or very serious. All these things may make it hard to identify the condition. Yet it is important to **diagnose** asthma as soon as possible, so effective treatment can begin right away.

For a proper diagnosis, the first thing you need to do is go to the doctor. The doctor will ask questions about the illness and your family's medical history. Does anyone in your family have asthma or allergies? When did the breathing problems begin? What are the symptoms? How serious are they? When and where do they occur? How often do they occur? How long do they last? Does the problem get worse after crying, laughing, or exercising? Are you exposed to cigarette smoke, air pollution, or other irritants?

Did You Know...

Some kids develop asthma symptoms at night and then feel fine during the day. This can make it hard for a doctor who sees them only during the day to diagnose the condition.

Keep an Asthma Diary

You can help the doctor make a diagnosis by keeping a diary of your condition. Write down as much as you can about the problem. Make sure you enter the dates and times when problems occur with a complete description. What are the symptoms? What were you doing before they started?

An asthma diary will help the doctor and patient understand the illness better. That way the doctor can treat the condition more effectively.

The doctor will then give you a physical exam, starting with your nose to look for signs of allergy or upper respiratory infection. He or she will check your breathing with a stethoscope. This instrument is used to listen to your heart and lungs. It helps the doctor hear if they are working properly. But if you are not having any symptoms at that moment, your breathing will probably sound normal. Sometimes, if you are having serious breathing problems, the doctor may use a chest X-ray to see if the airways are blocked.

However, this test works best when it is taken while the patient is having breathing problems.

An asthma specialist may give the patient breathing tests using a **spirometer**. This instrument measures how much air flows in and out of the person's airways when he or she blows into a special tube. Then a patient is given medication that opens up airways. If the spirometer shows that the airflow is much better, this is more evidence that the person has asthma.

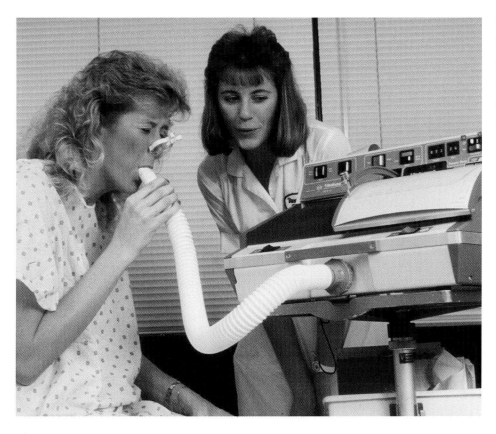

This woman is using a spirometer to measure the flow of air in her airways.

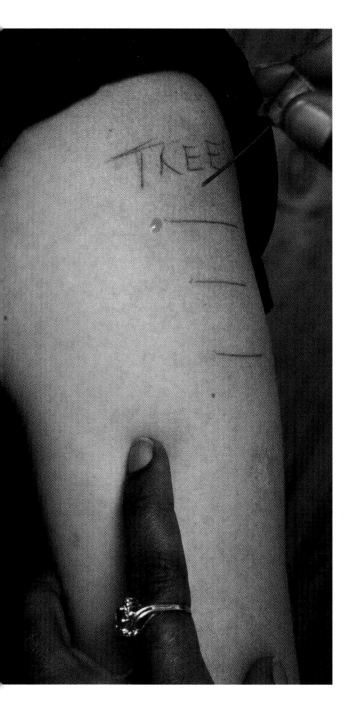

Since allergens are one of the most common triggers of asthma, allergy testing is an important tool for diagnosis. Skin testing is used to identify the allergens that may be causing the person's asthma attacks. Allergens are placed on skin that is scratched or pricked with a needle. Sometimes small amounts of an allergen solution are injected into the skin. If the skin is red and swollen within 15 minutes, you are sensitive to that allergen.

There are also special blood tests used to test for allergies. The **RAST test** measures the amounts of antibodies that are caused by specific allergens. For instance, if you have a special antibody for dust in your blood, then you are probably allergic to house dust.

Allergens are placed on scratches on the skin to test for allergic reactions.

This girl is measuring how fast the air flows out of her lungs with a peak flow meter.

There is one testing device that patients can use in their own homes—the **peak flow meter**. This device measures how fast air flows out of the lungs when a person exhales quickly. If the reading shows a drop in airflow, this could be a sign that an asthma attack is developing. The peak flow meter can actually show the early signs of an asthma attack even before the person is noticing breathing problems. This can help asthma patients treat the symptoms early, before they have a chance to get worse. The peak flow meter can also help to diagnose kids whose asthma occurs mostly at night.

Treating Asthma

There is no cure for asthma, but it can be controlled. Asthma patients need to work closely with their doctors to find a treatment plan that works best for them. Each person with asthma has different needs, so every treatment plan is different. With an effective treatment plan, people with asthma can live normal lives.

Asthma medications come in many forms, including pills, liquids, and injections. But inhalers are actually the most popular device people use for asthma treatment. That's because they are fast, easy, and handy. For severe attacks, people often use a hand-held inhaler called a **nebulizer**. A nebulizer sprays a mist of medication into the person's bronchial tubes. The drug works right there to open up the airways and relieve the symptoms.

Inhalers are easy to use and can be carried just about anywhere.

There are two main types of asthma medications: **bronchodilators** and anti-inflammatory drugs.

Bronchodilators are drugs that work by relaxing the muscles in the airways, allowing the narrowed airways to open up. Air can then flow in and out more easily, making it easier to breathe. Bronchodilators are often used to relieve symptoms just as they occur. But if the person's asthma is severe, he or she may need to take the bronchodilator regularly, even when there are no symptoms. This can prevent attacks before they happen.

Many doctors believe that it is most important to treat the main problem of asthma — inflammation of the airways. Anti-inflammatory drugs can do the job by reducing the swelling and twitchiness in the airways. These drugs are usually taken regularly, once or twice a day. Regular use of these drugs can help to make the airways less sensitive and less likely to start a reaction.

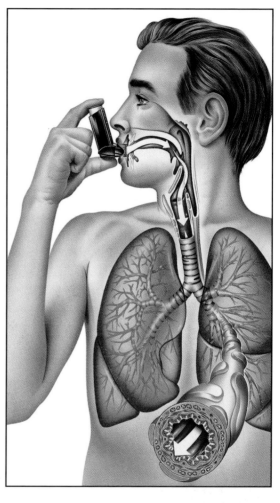

This diagram shows how bronchodilators move through the respiratory system and open airways.

What Are Steroids?

You may have heard about sports stars who take drugs called **steroids** to pump up their muscles. These drugs are dangerous and illegal. You may be surprised to learn, however, that some steroid drugs are used to treat asthma. These are not the same as the illegal steroids; they are anti-inflammatory drugs. When they are taken in the right amounts under a doctor's supervision, they are safe and effective.

How do you know what type of asthma medication you need and how much? Well, that depends on how severe the symptoms are and how often they occur. People with mild asthma may need fast-acting drugs that treat the symptoms on the spot.

People with a more serious case may need a long-term treatment plan. They may take asthma medications every day to control inflammation and symptoms. Eventually, the person will have fewer attacks. The person should continue to take medication, however, to keep the symptoms from coming back.

Asthma attacks that are caused by allergens can be controlled with medications that treat allergy symptoms.

Many people take **antihistamines**. Remember, histamine is the chemical that is released when the body is exposed to an allergen. It is the main cause of allergy symptoms. An antihistamine stops the harmful effects of histamine. Another kind of allergy drug, called **cromolyn sodium**, works by stopping the sensitive cells in the airways from reacting to allergens. They do not spill out histamine, and inflammation does not develop.

Scientists are working on an allergy treatment to block the antibodies that react with allergens. In studies of children and adults with asthma, many patients who got shots of the new treatment once or twice a month had fewer asthma attacks and needed less medication.

Decongestants are drugs that reduce swelling in the nasal passages. They help to clear a stopped-up nose so that you can breathe more easily.

Hot Stuff

Does eating chili or salsa make your nose run? If you have asthma, that may be a good thing. Scientists have found that hot peppers make the airways produce more fluid. This flushes out mucus and makes it easier to breathe.

Preventing Asthma Attacks

The only sure way to be asthma-free, or at least reduce your risk of asthma attacks, is to avoid the triggers. For example, if you are allergic to a particular food, you should not eat it. If you are allergic to dust mites, remove all rugs and curtains from your bedroom and use dust-proof covers on your mattress and pillow. Staying away from cigarette smoke can also help you avoid bringing on an asthma attack.

This man is using a hayfever helmet to avoid inhaling pollen and dust as he mows his lawn.

If your allergies come at certain times of the year, try to stay indoors during those times. This is especially helpful in the middle of the day when pollen counts are usually the highest. Keep the windows closed so that the pollen and mold spores do not get into your house. Use air-conditioning instead. An air cleaner with a HEPA filter can help reduce allergens in your house all year round. This device takes allergens out of the air.

One way to stop asthma attacks before they start is by taking asthma medication every day, as mentioned in the previous chapter. This is important if you need quick-relief medication more than two to three times a week.

People whose breathing problems are triggered by allergens can prevent asthma attacks by getting allergy shots. Each shot contains a tiny amount of an allergen.

HEPA filters help to remove allergens in the air.

When it is injected, some of the allergen gets into the blood and causes the body to make special antibodies for that allergen. These new antibodies are of a different kind from the ones that the body makes in allergic reactions. They react with the allergen and block it from reacting with allergy antibodies.

Each injection contains a little more of the allergen, and more blocking antibodies are made. After a while, there is enough of the blocking antibody to tie up the allergen and keep it from causing trouble. Your body is now desensitized, and the allergen no longer triggers an allergic reaction.

An allergy shot can help asthma patients avoid attacks.

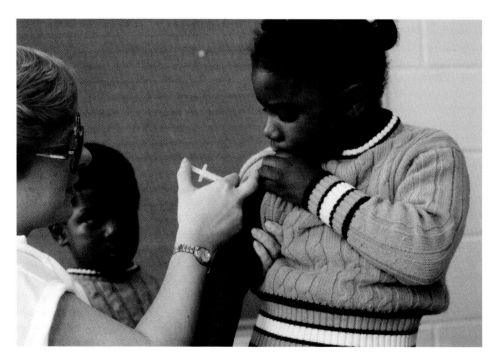

Glossary

allergen—a substance that causes an allergic reaction

allergy—an overreaction of the immune system to a normally harmless substance

alveoli (sing. **alveolus**)—the tiny air sacs in the lungs where gas exchange takes place

antibodies—special proteins produced by white blood cells. Some antibodies help to kill germs.

antihistamine—a drug that stops the effects of histamine that produce allergy symptoms

asthma—a disease in which the air passages in the lungs become inflamed, making breathing difficult

bronchi (sing. **bronchus**)—the larger air tubes of the lungs

bronchioles—smaller air tubes of the lungs that branch off from the bronchi

bronchodilator—a drug that opens the airways during an asthma attack

bronchospasm—a sudden, brief narrowing of the muscles in the airway walls

cilia—tiny hairlike structures in the lining of the airways that move back and forth, sweeping foreign particles out and up to the throat

cromolyn sodium—an allergy drug that works by stopping the sensitive cells in the airways from reacting to allergens

dander—flakes of dead skin from animals

decongestant—a drug that reduces swelling in the breathing passages

diagnose—to identify a condition from its signs and symptoms

dust mites—microscopic bugs that feed on dead skin in dust

histamine—a chemical released in the body that causes tissues to become inflamed in an allergic reaction

immune system—the body's disease-fighting system, including white blood cells

inflammation—redness and swelling as a result of damage or an allergic reaction

larynx—voice box

lungs—two balloon-like organs used for breathing

mucus—a gooey liquid produced by cells in the lining of the nose and breathing passages

nebulizer—a device that turns liquid into a spray; a type of inhaler

peak flow meter—a hand-held device that measures how fast air flows out of the lungs when a person exhales quickly

pharynx—throat

RAST test—a blood test for specific kinds of antibodies to show sensitivity to particular allergens

respiratory system—the organs involved in breathing, from the nose to the lungs

sensitization—development of an allergy after repeated exposure to an allergen

spirometer—a machine that measures how much air goes in and out of a person's airways

steroid—a type of anti-inflammatory drug

trigger—a substance or condition (such as dust or a cold) that brings on an asthma attack

trachea—the windpipe; breathing tube that connects the nose to the bronchi

wheeze—a whistling sound heard when a person breathes through narrowed airways

white blood cells—jelly-like blood cells that can move through tissues and are an important part of the body's defenses. Some white blood cells eat germs and clean up bits of damaged cells and dirt.

Learning More

Books

Adams, Francis V. *The Asthma Sourcebook: Everything You Need to Know*. Los Angeles, CA: Lowell House, 1998.

Hyde, Margaret O. and Elizabeth H. Forsyth. *Living with Asthma*. New York: Walker & Company, 1995.

Landau, Elaine. *Allergies (Understanding Illness)*. New York: Twenty-First Century Books, 1995.

Mitchell, Barbara. *Zooallergy: A Fun Story About Allergy and Asthma Triggers*. Valley Park, MO: JayJo Books, 1996.

Ostrow, William and Vivian. *All About Allergies*. New York: Lodestar Books, 1993.

Peacock, Judith. *Asthma (Perspectives on Disease and Illness)*. New York: Lifematters Press, 2000.

Silverstein, Alvin, Virginia Silverstein, & Laura Silverstein Nunn. *Asthma*. Springfield, NJ: Enslow Publishers, Inc., 1997.

Silverstein, Alvin, Virginia Silverstein, & Laura Silverstein Nunn. *Allergies*. Danbury, CT: Franklin Watts, 1999.

Weiss, Jonathan H. *Breathe Easy: Young People's Guide to Asthma*. Washington, DC: Magination, 1994.

Organizations and Online Sites

American College of Allergy, Asthma & Immunology
85 West Algonquin Road, Suite 550
Arlington Heights, IL 60005
http://www.allergy.mcg.edu/
This site includes "Kid's Asthma Check" which involves a number of questions to help kids identify signs of asthma.

Asthma
http://www.asthma.org.uk/
This site is provided by the National Asthma Campaign. It includes a special kids' section called "Kid Zone," which has lots of easy-to-understand information all about asthma.

Asthma Basics
http://kidshealth.org/parent/medical/lungs/asthma_basics_prt.htm
This site has general information about asthma.

Just for Kids: Growing Up with Asthma
http://www.aaaai.org/public/just4kids/kurt_grote.stm
This site includes a personal account of asthma written by an Olympic athlete named Kurt Grote.

National Jewish Center for Immunology and Respiratory Medicine
1400 Jackson St.
Denver, CO 80206
1-800-552-5864
http://www.njc.org/
This site includes the "Asthma Wizard" who gives kids information about asthma in a fun, easy-to-understand way.

Index

About the Authors

Dr. Alvin Silverstein is a professor of biology at the College of Staten Island of the City University of New York. **Virginia B. Silverstein** is a translator of Russian scientific literature. The Silversteins first worked together on a research project at the University of Pennsylvania. Since then, they have produced 6 children and more than 180 published books for young people.

Laura Silverstein Nunn, a graduate of Kean College, has been helping with her parents' books since her high-school days. She is the coauthor of more than 50 books on diseases and health, science concepts, endangered species, and pets. Laura lives with her husband Matt and their young son Cory in a rural New Jersey town not far from her childhood home.